TURNAROUND

THROUGH   INSPIRATION

DEDICATION: This book was written to demonstrate to the world, my wife, my parents, and especially my children that it is never too late to realize your dream. My mom who is an Alzheimer's patient returned to college at 62 years of age and completed it. Demonstrating to me that you can never be too old to realize your dream. I also dedicate this book to my loving wife who told me that this dream would materialize. She stood by me from beginning to the end. It was a pleasure to have her by my side with constant support and encouragement. I do not want to forget Mr. Obi Odiakosa who encouraged me to stay on task and to completion. And a special thanks to my father who instilled the work ethic in all of his children. Remember inspirational words will take you to positive places.

SPECIAL NOTE

This book is intended as an inspirational book only. The information given is designed to inspire you, encourage you, and show you the importance and power of positive words. You will find well thought out words and poetic grammar within the body of this work, to make you think. There are no specific companies, organizations, or authorities, who has influenced the authors thoughts and words. Whether you are just starting a new company, just starting college, or just starting the first grade. This book is designed as a spiritual tool to assist you in making some of life's tough decisions. Most important you will learn that a positive mindset can inspire you to do things that you may have thought impossible.

COPYRIGHT © 2020 by Erwin Burley, Writer and Poet

ALL RIGHTS RESERVED

All rights reserved. No part of this book may be reproduced or transmitted in any form or by any means, electronic or mechanical. This includes photocopying or recording by any information storage or retrieval system, without written permission from the author. The inspirational quotes in this book were designed to be helpful. The author nor the publisher shall not have any liability to any person or entity with respect to any loss or damage caused or alleged to be caused directly or indirectly by the information contained in this book.

TABLE OF CONTENTS

DEDICATION

SPECIAL NOTE

AUTHORS COMMENTS

COPYRIGHT

Chapter One: A Spiritual Journey

Chapter Two: The Almighty We Praise

Chapter Three: Secrets for a Successful life

Chapter Four: A Message of Good News

Chapter Five: The Roadblocks of Life

Chapter Six: So, You Think You are being Held Back

Chapter Seven: Days and Nights Pass Quickly

Chapter Eight: The Storms and the Rain

Chapter Nine: Things You Do Not Want to Do

Chapter Ten: When Two Hearts are Joined

Chapter Eleven: The Word of The Almighty will be Fulfilled

Chapter Twelve: The Lessons of Life

Chapter Thirteen: No Apology

Chapter Fourteen: Things that Appear as Adversity

Chapter Fifteen: Afflictions and Addictions

Chapter Sixteen: The Unexpected

Chapter Seventeen: The Center of All Affairs

Chapter Eighteen: The Almighty's Revelations

Chapter Nineteen: Inspiration and Goodness

Chapter Twenty: Misinformation

Chapter Twenty - One: Sacrifice

Chapter Twenty-Two: Form Your World

Chapter Twenty-Three: Concerned with Our Concerns

Chapter Twenty-Four: Never Fear Emotional Pain

Chapter Twenty -Five: Personality

Chapter Twenty-Six: Storms of Life

Chapter Twenty-Seven: Spiritual People

Chapter Twenty-Eight: Conversation

Chapter Twenty-Nine: The Test

Chapter Thirty: Spiritual Poems

Chapter Thirty-One: DIRECTION OF THE ALMIGHTY

Chapter Thirty-Two: Experience His love

Chapter Thirty-Three: Toxic Circumstances

Chapter Thirty-Four: Signs from The Almighty

Chapter Thirty-Five: Attention

Chapter Thirty-Six: Become Better

Chapter Thirty-Seven: Stay Healthy

Chapter Thirty-Eight: Your Destiny

Chapter Thirty-Nine: The World's Illness

Chapter Forty: Stop and Think

Chapter Forty-One: Arrogance

Chapter Forty-Two: Doing Good

Chapter Forty-Three: The Earth's Revolutions

Chapter Forty-Four: Nothing Going your Way

Chapter Forty-Five: Assurance from the Book

Chapter Forty-Six: Life is Serious

Chapter Forty-Seven: Never Forget the Almighty

Chapter Forty-Eight: The Almighty's Will and Plan

Chapter Forty-Nine: Enjoy your Life

Chapter Fifty: Messages with Clarity

Chapter Fifty-One: Be Prepared for Trials

Chapter Fifty-Two: No Weapon Formed Against You

Chapter Fifty-Three: Honor that is Due

Chapter Fifty-Four: Create a Universal Plan

Chapter Fifty-Five: Life's Difficulties

Chapter Fifty-Six: Truth and Falsehood

Chapter Fifty-Seven: Stand your Spiritual Ground

Chapter Fifty-Eight: A True Spirit of Service

Chapter Fifty-Nine: Hold on to your True Identity

Chapter Sixty: Simple Rules of Etiquette

Chapter Sixty-One: Think About the Universe

Chapter Sixty-Two: Through a New Door

Chapter Sixty -Three: Road to a Good Life

Chapter Sixty-Four: The Man who Worships the Almighty

Chapter Sixty-Five: Do not Bury your Ability

Chapter Sixty- Six: Share the Good News

Chapter Sixty- Seven: In Matters of Day and Night

Chapter Sixty-Eight: Spiritual Grace

Chapter Sixty-Nine: A Better Teacher

Chapter Seventy: Something Wonderful in the Universe

Chapter Seventy- One: Do you Need a word

Chapter Seventy-Two: When we are Running Hard in the Race

Chapter Seventy-Three: Always Moving with a Purpose

Chapter Seventy- Four: As the Clouds Move so High in the Sky

Chapter Seventy-Five: Do not Miss an Opportunity

Chapter Seventy-Six: Although You may not be a Prophet

Chapter Seventy-Seven: The Greatest Principles

Chapter Seventy-Eight: The Gift of the Almighty

Chapter Seventy-Nine: To the Almighty we Pray

Chapter Eighty: Being Real

Chapter Eighty-One: Never Forsake the Truth

Chapter Eighty-Two: Where you Put your Eyes

Chapter Eighty-Three: Grace and Favor

Chapter Eighty-Four: No More Emotional Pain

THE AUTHORS COMMENTS

The AUTHOR: Sends greetings to the world in hopes that the world will benefit in a small or great way from this book, which is now your book. Remember that words have a way of revealing your thoughts, your intentions, and inner secrets of the heart. Our goal was too also demonstrate how words can affect our lives. Words have been used as the catalyst to blind the minds of men, or too enlighten the minds of men. It is imperative that we remain actively involved in our past, present, and future. Therefore, we will safeguard and protect our histories thereby strengthening ourselves, our families, and our communities. The author's objective is enlightenment. Thus, he speaks to you through deep poetic terminology. So, that you will be able to recognize that you are truly a spiritual person on a spiritual journey, and hopefully on a spiritual road.

TITLE: TURNAROUND THROUGH INSPIRATION

A SPIRITUAL JOURNEY

A SPIRITUAL journey is specifically dated with laws and rules which have been mandated. But with our devotion and determination we should be elated. Our devotion to the Almighty is clearly demonstrated.

Yes, I am glowing because the grace of the Almighty is overflowing. Something powerful, something that will keep you going. Receiving direction and enjoying divine protection.

Yes, I have the keys to the spiritual world with a special story to tell. I have survived freed from a living hell. The Almighty took me from the world and introduced me to the drum of a new sound. A place where truth could be found and planted my feet on solid ground.

THE ALMIGHTY WE PRAISE

The Almighty we praise and bless his holy name. And by his power you became. He is deserving of all fame. Thus, continue to proclaim his holy name.

In matters of the heart let there be no negligence. The heart is the center of feeling and intelligence. Pray to the Almighty to remove any negative elements. Therefore, moving forward with confidence.

When the Almighty sends us in a particular direction, it is a path for our own protection. There is no need for correction. For this path is one of perfection.

SECRETS FOR A SUCCESSFUL LIFE

The Almighty has secrets for a successful life. Giving you instructions on how to treat your wife. HE has given us the power to apologize. Helping you spiritually to survive, always putting spiritual things first. Learn to prioritize.

Stand firm in your faith like the mountains that do not change from day to day. Avoid evil that spreads like the darkness of night, causing you to lose your way. Look to heavenly guidance that leads to a path where there is light each day.

When things become difficult turn to the Almighty and be quiet and still. Even though the whole world appears to be going uphill, you will hear his voice, thus follow his will.

A MESSAGE OF GOOD NEWS

The Almighty in his mercy always sends a message, a warning, and good news and through faith we can always receive spiritual views. Thus, choose the path where we can be first in sharing this good news.

Let us commit ourselves to the care of the Almighty, and with faith all will be well. No doubt, no insecurities, just a success story to tell.

Use your abilities that the Almighty has given you. You are capable, you are powerful, you are strong, and to him you belong. Be the best you can be and strengthen the relationship with yourself. Only then will you be able to help someone else.

THE ROADBLOCKS OF LIFE

When we try to better our lives the roadblocks of life will present obstacles, limitations, and setbacks, making it difficult to survive.
However, you will be successful if you hold to your faith in the Almighty and continue to strive.

Many men are ungrateful, doing things that are hateful. No appreciation, no afterthought, loving only things that are bought. Stop, look, and listen. Learn to be faithful doing things which are graceful. Turn to the Almighty the creator of the world who is never unfaithful.

Consider yourself blessed. Thousands of people die every day. You are blessed to be alive so enjoy your stay. Turn to the Almighty with thanks and pray. Yes, we are grateful to be alive to see another day.

SO, YOU THINK THAT YOU ARE BEING HELD BACK

If you think you have it bad, and are being held back, think about people who are in other countries under constant attack. Where families are separated and that is a fact. Turn to the Almighty and be grateful where you are.

Do not waste time pursuing that which is wrong. That which brings no blessing, nor does it put in your heart a spiritual song. Do not waste time on that which is worthless and only carries you along. Pray and reach out to the Almighty because there is where you belong.

Pray to see spiritual things clearly. For failure to do so could affect you severely. Seek guidance through prayer and do it sincerely. Thus, you will experience the mercy of the Almighty who loves you dearly.

DAYS AND NIGHTS PASS QUICKLY

As our days and nights pass us quickly, we must learn to understand ourselves completely. Adhere to the words of the Almighty strictly. Which will give us a life of victory.

Every day is a day to give thanks. Hopefully, this day will help you fill in the blanks. Enjoy the family, renew relationships, renew friendships, and fill up your spiritual bank. Learn to be appreciative and forgiving. And to the Almighty always give thanks.

Cultivate your good qualities, extend hospitality, work on your personality, live your best, and accept reality. Pray to the Almighty and do it constantly. And you will have success and live abundantly.

THE STORM AND THE RAIN

Although, in this life we experience the storm and the rain. Sometimes difficulties, hardships, and emotional pain. Continue steadfast, firm, and determined we must remain. Pray to the Almighty and he will help you maintain.

There are many things in this world that will attract you. And some of those will distract you. You must take spiritual action. Turn to the Almighty and find true satisfaction, enjoying a heavenly reaction.

One more day to be serious and practice what is right. And day after day the Almighty will show you the way.

THINGS YOU DON'T WANT TO DO

Yes, it is difficult to do things that we do not want to do. However, we must continue to push through. The prophets of old did it, and they had difficulties too. Reach out to the Almighty and you will make it through.

Although every day may not be a day of joy, nor go according to plan. Remain focused on the Almighty and continue to take your stand. With knowledge that he has the ultimate plan. And continues to bless us again and again.

When dedicated to that which is right, temptations we must fight. Pray to the Almighty to increase your spiritual light.

WHEN TWO HEARTS ARE JOINED

When two hearts are joined life can become a pleasure. When two minds are joined learning can become a treasure. When dedicated to that which is right our blessings will be in full measure.

When the Almighty speaks, you will not be in doubt as to what you think. The word of the Almighty is a powerful drink. Transforming your soul keeping you focused on the eternal goal. And giving you peace as each day unfolds.

Success comes with a price and sometimes a heavy sacrifice. Thus, turn to the Almighty in prayer and seek the best advice.

THE WORD OF THE ALMIGHTY WILL BE FULLFIELD

The word of the Almighty will be fulfilled. With truth there is no falsehood, and this is very clear. And with truth he brings blessings which are never misunderstood. With falsehood there is lies, deceit, and confusion, and never anything good.

With every day that begins we have an opportunity to ask for forgiveness for our sins. Never forget the promise to the Almighty that you made back then. A wonderful day when true life begins. Remaining a believer to the very end.

There are many things that we need and want to do.

Continue to be patient and patience will see you through. Yes, at times it may be uncomfortable to you. However, remain steadfast and firm. And through the Almighty your hopes and dreams will come true.

THE LESSONS OF LIFE

The lessons we learn in life are for guidance and protection. The trial placed before us by the Almighty is to give us direction. To strengthen us and keep us safe until we see paradise, our day of perfection.

The Almighty deserves our exclusive devotion. A way of life that is rewarding and not a notion. Continue to serve him remaining on a path that keeps us in motion. Moving as the river which flows constantly. Always seeking knowledge from the depths of the ocean abundantly.

Always beware of those who invent falsehoods to lead you astray. Those who do not realize the seriousness of each day. Although some allow deception to block their path that leads to the spiritual way. Protect yourself call on the Almighty and do not delay.

NO APOLOGY

You do not owe the world an apology for being who you are. The Almighty has created you and made you a star. However, the world will point out your scar. But it is not important because you were designed to go far. Continue to soar being who you are.

Do not become a slave to the economy, although it is important to protect your progeny. Life is serious it is not a comedy. So, establish something with spiritual harmony.

The Almighty gives us parables to make things clear. Therefore, no need to experience fear. Be strong and be faithful, and as believers always be sincere.

THINGS THAT APPEAR AS ADVERSITY

With all things that appear as adversity, continue to believe which will relieve the complexity. You can find happiness, pleasure, and peace which is your manifest destiny. And yes, Satan will continue testing me. And prayers to the Almighty will continue protecting me.

Praise the Almighty for another day of guidance, understanding, and wisdom the spiritual way. Time to be serious no time for amusement and play. The way to the straight path is open today.

Many look to men for guidance. However, with you and I, with man we can never be in compliance. Because with the Almighty there exists a higher guidance, one with the perfect science. So, with this we must form an alliance.

AFFLICTIONS AND ADDICTIONS

In the face of affliction, addictions, and deceptive transactions. There is a path that provides relief. One where there are no contradictions, only peaceful conditions and spiritual position. With paradise the final transition.

When you believe in the Almighty, he will believe in you. When you grow close to him, he will grow closer to you. When you become his friend, he will be your friend to the very end. With power to give your life again.

Seek the Almighties protection, his guidance, and his direction. Never let go of this powerful spiritual connection. Remember we fight against unseen forces and men. Those who attack from without and from within. But remember we have protection that knows no end.

THE UNEXPECTED

The unexpected can catch you totally by surprise. And some of your principles you might compromise. This could lead to your eternal, or temporary demise. Therefore, always prioritize. Stay awake, seek spiritual laws from the Almighty and you will grow in size.

Remember that time is timeless. But with people our time is limited. Therefore, follow the straight path and remain in that interested. And as time continues to pass with help from the Almighty, we will have our paradise certificate.

The Almighty is the symbol of all guidance. You can hear his voice when you sit and meditate in silence. You do not have to be a professor, or a scholar of science, always be humble never in defiance.

THE CENTER OF ALL AFFAIRS

The Almighty is the center of all affairs, deserving all praise. He can provide for you materially, and spiritually. Lifting you up all your days. So, to him we continue to worship, we continue to praise.

The word of the Almighty illuminates the mind. And his peace in his word you will find. And this will continue until the end of time. So, seek out those things which are divine. And the spiritual mountains continue to climb.

The righteous man has no reason to fear. He is aware that the Almighties truth is clear. A powerful defense that the enemy cannot come near.

THE ALMIGHTIES REVELATION

When the revelation of the Almighty, breaks through the darkness of the human soul. You will become a new person you will become bold. Because of the truth as it unfolds. So, remember the history of old, and from there set your goal.

It makes no difference what man may say, or what men may do. The word of the Almighty will forever hold true. And this truth will prevail overlooking no detail. Weighing with a perfect set of scales.

To become rich spiritually, mentally, and physically. These are priceless in health and wealth. Look to the Almighty, do not look to anyone else. And do not become deaf. And you will be standing the only one left.

INSPIRATION AND GOODNESS

With the Almighty comes inspiration and goodness. No madness or darkness, his blessings and forgiveness are countless. The possibilities that he extends for success or endless. Never forget, his blessings are tremendous.

We were created to do things that other people cannot do. Each of us doing things different, doing things new. Some like red others like blue. Remember to always be true to you.

Life without a plan brings nothing to a man. Although he lives in a prosperous land, he has nothing on which to stand. However, with the Almighty he will multiply like grains of sand.

MISINFORMATION

Whether it be social media, misinformation, slander, and, lies. These have been used for centuries by the enemy to divide. Show yourself worthy of the Almighty. Never allowing division in these respects and we will be multiplying.

The righteous man will find the Almighty enough for all the protection he needs. And all the happiness that he can ever imagine. Continue to be led by him although true worship is not in fashion.

 Remember some of us may be criticized and abused, spit up on and used. But the spiritual life we continue to choose. We are not offended, nor do we misuse, for our relief is due to the Almighty, and our belief in him is true.

SACRIFICE

Remain ready for prayer and sacrifice. But there is nothing easy or simple in this life. However, doing good always will assist you in lengthening your days. And the Almighty we continue to praise.

We must continue to be spiritually prepared. Remain innocent and sincere because a tremendous day of judgment is near. It will come suddenly and unexpected, although the Almighty will direct it.

It is by spiritual effort and long preparation through a good life will one rise above. And learn how to show sincere love, remaining innocent like the dove.

FORM YOUR WORLD

Shape and form your world the way you want it to be. And continue to grow just like a tree. And although it may appear to be slow keep it moving and you will continue to go.

Somewhere someone is inquiring about death. Yes, I am thanking the Almighty for another day and for each breath. Continue to move forward, and we will find a place of rest, and pass each spiritual test.

Continue to keep the name of the Almighty in your thoughts. And in his name wars have been fought. In his name we have been taught. So, hold on to him and you will not become distraught.

CONCERNED WITH OUR CONCERNS

You should always be concerned with your concerns. However, never worry because it does not solve anything. Never doubt the vast realities of that which you do not see, and many things will remain a mystery. You cannot see hope although it is there for you and me. And that alone is one reality.

Remember to remain positive today. And even if trouble comes your way, turn to the Almighty and continue to pray and you will Have a brighter day.

The Almighty can expose every fact of life, the known and the unknown. In that which is unknown there may be something good; something that can be shown.

NEVER FEAR

One can never have victory if there is fear. Continue to fight with all your might. And continue to pray and you will pass the test. Build your structure high, and strong like the eagle in his nest. And we will find victory, in this earthly contest.

The Almighty rewards us and gives us success, only wanting for his servants that which is the best. With the promise of paradise, eternal truth, peace, and rest.

Do not build your life around material wealth. Focus on your spiritual health because when you look in the mirror you will only see yourself.

PERSONALITY

Personality the inner and real self. Look in the mirror there is no need to look anywhere else. Do not put your wealth of knowledge on the shelf. Share it with others so, they too may be helped.

Do not give in to the world's accusations. Remain steadfast with spiritual expectations. And the Almighties spiritual explanations will lead us to paradise our final destination.

Great powers rise and fall. Some can help you, and some cannot help you at all. But with the help of the Almighty his power surpasses all. Pay attention and listen to his voice and answer his call. And you will have power to conquer all.

STORMS OF LIFE

There may be storms in your life as powerful as hurricane force. Pray to the Almighty your life will stay on course. Continue to stay focused and spiritual laws continue to enforce. And that will be the best recourse.

The Almighty makes the wrong take flight and continues to turn night into light. But with the spiritual life there is a light where every street becomes bright. So, continue to read, continue to write. With these you will enhance your life.

Blueprint your life the spiritual way and you will find that it makes for a better day. So, I write this message hoping you can see that the spiritual life will guide you to your true destiny.

SPIRITUAL PEOPLE

As spiritual people we never stop giving, never stop living. Remember life is worth living. Serving the Almighty is our obligation. Do so filled with determination. Therefore, no one can bring us humiliation. With help from the one above we as spiritual people can change the nation.

A shout out to those behind bars. Many of you are real superstars. Stay spiritually fit it and it will take you far. Remember there's people thinking about you, we know where you are.

Always with the Almighty does a believer have trust. And you will have his support on the day of judgment. Everyone coming forward with the report. It will not be a time for play or sport. Everyone standing in the Most Highs court.

CONVERSATION

Be careful with conversation because it can cause a catastrophic situation. It can cause widespread condemnation. Cling to the words of the Almighty which is the best information and it always comes with a concise confirmation.

At times one must continue to endure storms of tremendous pressure. Troubles and problems can be so great that we cannot even measure. Hold on to the Almighty read his word and be comforted by the spiritual treasure.

So now it is time to pick up the pen and write a message about the Almighty again. The creator of all creation. Soon to bring peace to all the nations. Stay focused in prayer and it will change your situation.

THE TEST

Remember each day comes with the test. We are all running a race which is a contest. With health from the Almighty we can perform at our very best. And we are not overly stressed we are extremely blessed.

A house on a firm foundation is built to last. But a house on Sandy soil will not last it will crumble and turn to Ashes and take you fast. So, live a spiritual life and find grace, it will put a smile on your face. The Almighty is not controlled by time or space and it is not important what color are race. Do your best and pass the test.

Spiritual views are often discussed based on truth, based on that which is just. To be led by the spirit this is a must. Life with the Almighty you can trust, so spiritual views I continue to discuss.

SPIRITUAL POEMS

Spiritual poems to get you going and moving in the right direction. Under the direction of the Almighty's guidance and protection. Do not give up, do not give in, do not permit Satan to trick you again. The Most High knows where you have been, and he has fortified you so that you will win.

There is no reason to compare yourself to another. For every true believer is either your sister or your brother. So, there is no need to compare it is only a snare. And remember with the Almighty he is in control of every affair.

Remember the world is a place that will support you in the morning and forget you in the afternoon but do not be sad, do not embrace the gloom. Because the Almighty brings life into every room.

THE DIRECTION OF THE ALMIGHTY

From the direction of the Almighty comes equality, justice, and righteousness. Soon inequality, injustice, an evil will be gone. We will be serving the Most High who sits on his glorious throne. And he will provide for us our eternal home.

You can be no one better than yourself. Remember we must also forgive ourselves. When self-forgiveness is displayed others will forgive you. And with forgiveness you will become a witness to new hopes, new goals, and dreams of sweetness. Seeking the Almighty's forgiveness with meekness.

The Almighty has given us spiritual books to learn how to fulfill our mission. So, when doing spiritual things, and things for others, do it with the right intentions. So, that in the end we will be found among those, that he will make mention.

EXPERIENCE HIS LOVE

The Almighty will allow you to experience his love. A radiant light coming from above. And as I write this spiritual report, I pray for your love and continued support.

The Almighty is the means to cure to all mental and physical pain. Daily prayers will help us to maintain. Continue to engage in faithful service, with the hope of everlasting gain.

With the Almighty we have the keys to the spiritual world. This includes the heart of every little boy and every little girl. So, use these keys to do what is right. Whether it be day, or whether it be night.

TOXIC CIRCUMSTANCES

When a situation, circumstance, or person, becomes toxic we must cut them off from our circle of friends. For many of them follow wicked trends. Against such people and toxic circumstances, we must defend. And keeping your distance is a way to cleanse.

Time and unforeseen circumstances befall us all. And for those of us who do not want to fall, to the Almighty we must continue to call. And then, you will be standing tall. Do not settle for less when you can have it all.

Divine wisdom is the solution to spiritual problems through revelation. The Almighty has provided the revelation that brings healing to your situation. The knowledge may come from a baby, a little boy, or a little girl. Knowledge comes from all over the world. Thus, truth from the Almighty will be hurled.

SIGNS FROM THE ALMIGHTY

In seeking signs of the Almighty's guidance, it may come in the form of silence. It may come in a force of science and with his signs we must form an alliance and work hard to live in compliance.

Every discipline is within the Almighty's principles. These are not fictional nor minimal. Although, mystical rising to the pinnacle.

There is a word called Salvation to receive it you must have patience. And the Almighty thinks of you, we have not been forsaken. Despite the crisis, hold on and do not let your faith be shaken.

ATTENTION

Be careful about the type of attention you receive. The wrong idea could be conceived. The Almighty wants us to focus our attention on truth, things you can believe.

Do not fear your destiny has already been written. The Almighty has said avoid that which is forbidden. Even those things that you think are hidden, and your success will be given.

The sands of time never stop. They continue to run. Time cannot be understood by men, it is a spiritual phenomenon. But if you endure to the end you will be have won.

BECOME BETTER

As things become worse than ever, we as believers must become better. Able to withstand the pressure from all kinds of weather. Holding on to the word of the Almighty as your guiding letter.

The Almighty is the ultimate reality. Thus, with him there is finality. Practice that which is good and always maintain your morality.

Let there be no division in your household. Pray to the Almighty and together the family will reach the goal, and to him continue to hold.

STAY HEALTHY

Are we seeing the fulfillment of scripture where we will not be able to buy or sell? Because for many this life has become a living hell. Pray to the Almighty that you will be able to, stay healthy, well, and continue to excel.

In this life or you gaining or are you pointing the finger and blaming? Are you taking life seriously? Are you gaining? Build a relationship with Almighty and true life you will be claiming.

Opportunity rarely presents itself when it does make the best of it. The account is not taken now but will be taken in the end.

YOUR DESTINY

Do not fear, your destiny has already been written. The Almighty has said avoid that which is forbidden. Question, even those things that you think are hidden, and your success will be given.

Only see grace and forgiveness, truth be told this is spiritual business. And the Almighty in his mercy will forgive us with swiftness.

The Almighty has created all things. And to his word forever cling. And yes, you have free will but never be a puppet on a string.

THE WORLDS ILLNESS

Only the Almighty has the answer to this illness that has struck the world like cancer. Stay strong in your belief and do what is right. And continue to pray day and night. Thus, this is your spiritual enhancer.

Let there be an inspirational turn around in your life. And you will no longer live with strife.

Becoming the best husband becoming the best wife.

Continue to listen to the Almighty with his powerful message. In the trials and tribulations of life you will avoid a severe wreckage. Start new today and enjoy all the spiritual successes.

STOP AND THINK

Remember always take time to stop and think. And from a spiritual perspective we must drink. And with the Almighty continue to stay linked. And then you can be certain that all things are in sync.

Help us to see things clear and to always be aware that the Almighty is near, and his blessings are everywhere. Think about it.

Anyone who preaches the truth should lead a noble life. And if you want to talk the talk, walk the walk. You may have lots of money, but true love of the Almighty cannot be bought.

ARROGANCE

Be careful with arrogance because you have the power at the present. Did you not know that being humble and striving to serve the Almighty is more pleasant?

In the Almighty we can trust to give us a lifestyle which is robust. A lifestyle which is just, giving everlasting life which is a plus. So, know that in him we can forever trust.

The true believers are those who have faith in the Almighty, and in the future. With these beliefs you can accomplish that which is super. And in spiritual things you will be a producer.

DOING GOOD

Doing good cannot be submerged. Doing good is always urged. And serving the Almighty is a life we have preferred. And in doing so your life will be preserved.

Think about your future and your destiny. With the Almighty you can plan successfully. Be confident and he will provide every necessity. And that is the spiritual recipe.

The tree is free to grow, the sea is free to flow, and the air is free to blow. Freedom comes with a price. And this we all know. True freedom comes from the Almighty thus to him you should go.

THE EARTHS REVOLUTIONS

Remember the Almighty and how he is caused the earth to turn with powerful revolutions. So, continue to progress and make positive contributions. Keep revolving and evolving and when there is a problem seek positive solutions.

Do not focus on thoughts that are contradictory. Do not fall for the devil's trickery. Stand with the Almighty. Declare and decree victory.

There are many hidden causes of trials and tribulations. Thus, make the Almighty your foundation. And continue to pray for inspiration, and one day soon, you will reach your desired destination.

NOTHING GOING YOUR WAY

There are days when it appears that nothing is going your way. It appears that you are losing more each day. It is only a trick of the devil.

Thus, to the Almighty continue to pray and you will see a brighter day.

One day soon traces of inequality, injustice, darkness, and evil will be gone. And the Almighties believers will not stand alone. Good deeds they have sown and spiritual growth they have shown.

Use the gifts of the Almighty and esteem them. They will bring you honor and blessings. Glorify him, and your cup will run over the brim, with the light that will never become dim.

ASSURANCE FROM THE BOOK

Assurance from the book that makes things clear. The book that assures us that he is near. Therefore, we have no reason to fear.

Continue to pray to the Almighty several times a day. Be very careful with the words you use, watch what you say. There is more to life than amusement and play. Bless yourself and bless your day, doing things the spiritual way.

Right and wrong, good and evil, or incompatible. And there can be no compromise. Never can you rationalize these as being equal. Stay separated from the upheaval. Keep your vision clear as the eagle, always living as the Almighties people.

LIFE IS SERIOUS

Did you take life serious today? Or was it amusement and play? Did you do what was right? Think about it tonight, think about doing right. Why? Remember doing wrong does not last long.

One more day to be serious and practice what is right, continuing to pray to the Almighty every day and every night. He will show you the way every day.

Who woke you up today? Who provided for you today? The Almighty provides for all according to his will and plan. And he can carry out his will. And a beautiful life for you he has planned.

NEVER FORGET THE ALMIGHTY

Never forget the Almighty he will never forget about you. We must never rely totally upon our own resources; so much as to forget spirituality.

Remember Abraham a faithful servant from men of old. His life may not have been perfect, but in every book his story is told.

The Almighty's universe is boundless. The night, the day, the sun, and the moon. Sometimes we cannot comprehend its relation to us. Try and be numbered with those who know, people who talk less but can show, not standing still, people on the go.

Life can be tough, although things may not be going the way you want them to go, you may succeed although the going be slow. Do not give up, do not give in, and do not give out. Changes we do go through, but the Almighty will always be true. And he will see you through.

THE ALMIGHTYS WILL AND PLAN

Whatever happens is the result of the Almighty's will and plan. He knows all things. And even in adversity keep your faith pure. Remember your victories are very near.

Your life has been built under the special instructions of the Almighty. To serve the special purpose it was intended to serve. Give yourself the best things. And always be conscious of your spiritual state, always observe.

You do not have any help besides the Almighty. He has helped you. He has helped me. Open your eyes so you can see his love. Praise him and blessings will come from above.

ENJOY YOUR LIFE

Enjoy your life. and keep on dreaming, dreaming, dreaming. For life is full of meaning, meaning, meaning!

The Almighty has given different types of enjoyment. Physical, social, mental, moral, and spiritual. His fruits are available for eating so why are you cheating? Life is full of meaning, enjoy your life and keep on dreaming.

The Almighty's kindness and mercy are different than that of men. It is one of Infinity. It will strengthen your mentality and increase your spirituality.

MESSAGES WITH CLARITY

Messages with clarity. Be careful with similarities. The Almighty will send you a clear message. Learn to read and remain in a state of purity. And you will be provided with security.

There are many things that you may want to do, many times our plans include others too. But remember pray to the Almighty and to your own self always remain true.

Man has been blessed with a limited free will. Pray to the Almighty and he will reveal all things for your life which are real. Thus, let your light shine with zeal.

BE PREPARED FOR TRIALS

When serving the Almighty be prepared for trials. Evil will always devise plots against those who choose to do right. Read, and pray to strengthen your place of abode, and continue to live by the spiritual code.

Remember the condition and position that you are in. Be aware of what motivates you and the endings you have in view. Therefore, with the Almighty spiritual blessings you will accrue.

The Almighty has created freshwater and saltwater they are joined yet remain separate. Although you are in the world remain separate from the world. Choose a good brother, choose a goodwife, and enjoy the rest of your life.

NO WEAPON FORMED AGAINST YOU

The Almighty has said no weapon formed against you shall prosper. Never give up, fight until the end, and new life for you will begin.

Trouble, trials, good days, bad days, ups and downs. Yes, the devil he is still around, soon the Almighty will destroy that clown. And the believers will have health and peace, in paradise safe and sound.

Spiritual service and endeavors are very necessary. Temptations and trials, they will help you carry. Spiritual things or not imaginary. Pray to the Almighty, keep it moving, and you will not become weary.

HONOR THAT IS DUE

Give the Almighty the honor that he is due. Only he alone can save you. And his word will be found true. So, practice that which he instructs you to do, and there will be prosperity for me and for you.

The Almighty has given you life so do not waste it. Saving yourself from disgrace. Be true to your own faith and goodness you will taste.

Receive your blessings because of the truth you have embraced.

The crossroads in life gives us a choice every day. Either good or bad. Our life is like a mirror reflecting the image of right or of wrong. Who do you want to please? Man will let you down. The Almighty will never let you down.

CREATE A UNIVERSAL PLAN

Start today with a universal plan. Choose a side. Be a real woman be a real man. Walk with the Almighty and respect you will command. Soon you will have the upper hand being victorious throughout the land.

Trust in the Almighty and do your best. And you will pass test after test. And that you cannot do, the Almighty can help you through. Victory is yours.

Follow the signs and the guidance of the Almighty. Look to his signs concerning your life these will lead you away from things that cause strife. Live in the present doing things that are excellent and with that be content.

LIFE'S DIFFICULTIES

You must not be frightened by life's difficulties. Use your faculties. Avoid all liabilities. Remember when engaging in spiritual activities you will find security.

To all men, and women of faith: It is important that we guard our conduct. And the conduct of our families and those near and dear to us. For the consequences

of a fall can be terrible. Remember separation from the Almighty will be unbearable.

We must be very careful about the things we do. Just let your record reflect that which is true. There will be something in the future that is very good for you.

TRUTH AND FALSEHOOD

There is a record kept of truth and falsehood. There is a record kept of right and wrong. Thus, live as you should. Always do good. Pray to the Almighty that his truth will be well understood.

The Almighty has created all things with purpose and design. And has given us a book with a way to live, and his laws have been defined. To give mankind a life that is divine. Live your life according to his design and let your light shine. Live the best life possible you deserve it. Protect your life preserve it.

In the twinkling of an eye the Almighty can give you success or failure. Thus, it is up to you to measure. Remember life is a treasure and living it to the fullest brings much pleasure.

STAND YOUR SPRITUAL GROUND

Stand your spiritual ground. And in the end truth will be found. Listen to the voice of the Almighty, truly a beautiful sound.

Purity of motives and purity of life are given to you by the Almighty to guide you to the right. Make your plans and keep your goal insight. Spiritual things continue to write. And you will reach spiritual heights.

May our prayers to the Almighty be about serious matters. Praying that our prayers be accepted and not rejected. For by our prayers we are protected. And by prayer into paradise we will be elected.

A TRUE SPIRIT OF SERVICE

Do you have a true spirit of service for the Almighty and man? When is the last time you gave someone a helping hand? Doing good when there is no demand. Do something great for someone today, do something grand.

The word of Almighty is a guide to show you the way. Do not be misled to the wrong path. Giving you the right formula as you do the math . It is easy because there is only one right path. So, walk the right path and avoid the world and its wrath.

Serve the Almighty according to the laws that he has established. Not something that we think is right. Remember our prayers each day and prayers throughout the night. They give strength and help us fight. And your life will continue moving right whether it is day or night.

HOLD ON TO YOUR TRUE IDENTITY

Hold onto your identity. Others want to choose your destiny. More than likely this is your worst enemy. Pray to the Almighty with intensity and continue to create your legacy.

There could be moments in your life where you are unsure of which path to take. Remember that there is a path filled with trouble, deception, and people who are fake. Make the right decision take the path of the Almighty and enter the paradise gate.

The lion meets all challenges head on and stands his ground. Be careful pray and stand your ground. And victory through the Almighty will be found.

SIMPLE RULES OF ETIQUETTE

Remember the keynote to the simple rules of etiquette. First self-respect and respect for all others, and respect for your spiritual sisters and brothers, never forgetting our mothers. And this rule applies to all cultures. A blessing from the Almighty a spiritual structure.

The Almighty's light is a reflected reality. Real charity, giving us clarity, a powerful mentality, a life of quality. Light from a true reality.

The highest and greatest gift of the Almighty is his revelation. With instruction he keeps our life under construction and saves us from destruction.

THINK ABOUT THE UNIVERSE

Think about the universe when it came into being. Why do you continue to doubt the power of the Almighty although you are seeing? The creation manifest itself, surely you are agreeing. And from wrong you should be fleeing, if you want spiritual well-being.

As the new day begins success will be yours. Keep it moving, keep it going, and you will make an awesome showing.

As one day ends and a new one begins. Pray to the Almighty and ask forgiveness for your sins. Seeking togetherness, bringing the family together again. And happiness forever, no limit no end.

THROUGH A NEW DOOR

As you go through a new door the spiritual life will give you more. More love, more hope, and blessings galore. Remain steadfast with the Almighty and be blessed forevermore.

I am content because my days are well spent. Studying the laws of the Almighty and doing good is my intent. Thus, remain in submission and into eternal life you will transition.

You have been given authority to do many things. And in some of these the Almighty does intervene. Although it is only for the best, teaching us to do that which is clean.

ROAD TO A GOOD LIFE

The road to a good life has been made clear. But the evil one has struck and planted fear. However, be of good cheer because the Almighty is near.

Our world a very special and beautiful land. However, even with our sorrows we still stand. So, look to the Almighty for his helping hand.

Success that comes from spiritual grace will put a happy smile on your face. And the Almighty will put you in a place where real love can be embraced.

THE MAN WHO WORSHIPS THE ALMIGHTY

The man who worships the Almighty and takes his revelations to heart; from the right path he will never depart. He will help others remain steadfast and get off to a good start, planting seeds of righteousness in their heart.

Live by the laws of the Almighty and exercise them constantly. And you will have a life and blessings more abundantly. Therefore, continue to pray constantly.

Seek that which is spiritual and may it be abundant. An increase of at least 100 and with the Almighty you will be triumphant.

DO NOT BURY YOUR ABILITY

Do not bury your ability. Seek the Almighty and enjoy his stability. Therefore, you will find permanent tranquility and enhance all of your abilities.

The earth is a wide expanse. Use its resources wisely and you will advance. Therefore, leave nothing to chance. Trust the Almighty and he will fortify your spiritual stance.

The Almighty can command the flowers to grow as mighty towers. Sending lifesaving showers and only he knows the day and the hour.

SHARE THE GOOD NEWS

Continue to share the good news, share the good life, with a loving wife. Find a true friend staying true to the end. The Almighty in his mercy always sends a message of warning. And through faithful men we receive good news and spiritual views. A path from where we can choose, so be first in sharing this good news.

Clear signs revealed by the Almighty are essential. They show who you really are and display your credentials. For we are raised in rank by knowledge. Get an education, and if need be go to college.

And with forgiveness you become a witness to new hope, to new goals, and dreams of sweetness. Fulfill every believer's engagement and your actions will make a statement. Yes, it is true others will experience amazement, and your heart will find contentment living under the Almighties arrangement.

IN MATTERS OF DAY AND NIGHT

In matters of day and night, sun and moon, life and death. We will find the Almighty most gracious, making the earth spacious. Therefore, trust him remember no need to be anxious.

Tricknology is not necessary for prosperity. Nor do we seek popularity. Focus on that which is right and be a cheerful giver in charity. And the Almighty will increase your posterity.

With correct thinking spiritual things are easily understood. The signs will appear clearly, and you will do good. And with the help of the Almighty you will easily see falsehood.

SPIRITUAL GRACE

Success comes with spiritual grace. And that will put a happy smile on your face. And the Almighty will put you in a place where real love can be embraced.

Power and strength have manifested itself through our descendants. And on the Almighty we can have 100 percent dependence. AND with that our blessings will be tremendous.
Do not be counted among those who are classified as material minded people. Among

those who lose focus and become feeble. But cling to the Almighty and with that you will remain gleeful.

A BETTER TEACHER

Learn to listen and be a better teacher. Avoid the evil one because he is a wicked creature. Hold onto that which is true and that which is right. And you will have strength to continue this fight. Praying to the Almighty day and night.

Do not be among those who will perish. Those who are not serious and living careless. Rather trust in the Almighty and in his truth always cherish.

Humble yourself and seek the Almighty's voice. Good, bad, right, or wrong light or darkness, you have a choice. Seek what is right and rejoice.

SOMETHING WONDERFUL IN THE UNIVERSE

There is something wonderful in the universe and it has no need to rehearse. It is a good thing to be involved in spiritual converse. Always moving forward and with the Almighty no need to reverse.

And for good, firmly take your stand. All the signs indicate that the hour is near at hand. Be aware that the Almighty has something great for you something planned.

So, have you considered the great dividend in making the Almighty your friend? He can help you with all things he can help you ascend. And your life he can extend.

DO YOU NEED A WORD?

Do you need a word something that will free your spirit and cause you to soar like a bird? Is it because of the truth that you heard or is it because your spirit the Almighty has stirred?

So, you say you want to teach, then you say you want to preach. Have you considered your speech? Pray to the Almighty and many you may reach.

When we think about spiritual success, we focus on all the things in which we have been blessed. We strive to do our best, and when doing so, the Almighty will help you accomplish the rest.

RUNNING HARD IN THE RACE

When we are running hard in the race you can be assured of the Almighty's grace and peace. Thus, when you think deeply there can be no better place. And you can be assured that when doing right you will pick up the pace.

As the world continues to spin on its own axis, people are everywhere with different things that they practice. Some can only see living in a world of blackness. Pray to the Almighty to deliver you, from the world's madness. Giving you gladness instead of sadness.

Although some move each day at a blazing speed remember constancy and patience will provide for your needs. Come and the Almighty will help you with every good deed.

ALWAYS MOVING WITH A PURPOSE

Always moving with a purpose, no spiritual thing can we purchase. Staying far from the world and its never-ending circus. Pray constantly to the Almighty to forever remain in his service.

In our heart we sing songs of joy. We reach out too little girls and little boys. Their lives are important it is not a toy. And through those whom the Almighty supports we can help them find joy.

Should problems and trouble arise, and others meet their demise, keep going, keep moving, and your faith do not compromise. The Almighty will help you maximize and strengthen your spiritual ties.

AS THE CLOUDS MOVE SO HIGH IN THE SKY

As the clouds move so high in the sky, we pray to the Almighty to open our spiritual eye, and with others we form allies. Working together to reach an everlasting prize.

When the Almighty shines his light things quickly go right. No need for fuss no need for fright. And his light shines even in the darkest of night. And when doing right, your world will become bright.

Be sure that you have the correct definition, then you will be empowered to understand your mission. And with spiritual things let there be no omission. Therefore, with the Almighty he will strengthen your ambition.

DO NOT MISS AN OPPORTUNITY

Do not miss an opportunity to do something positive for your community. And exercise maturity turning to the Almighty exclusively. And experience his security.

Fill up your spiritual account, it is not important the amount. Only the Almighty knows the count, and he knows that your heart is devout.

Be a spiritual instrument and active participant. And the Almighty will protect you from detriment, and false spiritual imprisonment. Now it is time for you to be free and live the best life spiritually.

ALTHOUGH YOU MAY NOT BE A PROPHET

Although you may not be a Prophet you are very able to make your spiritual deposit. And the Almighty will protect you from that which is catastrophic.

It is impossible for you to lose, because of a of life with the Almighty you choose. There will be spiritual and mental breakthroughs and an unbelievable amount of power will be yours to use.

Although we may see dark clouds and people falling in crowds. You can still hear the voice of the Almighty although it is silent and not loud. So be grateful because you are spiritually endowed.

THE GREATEST PRINCIPLES

The spiritual books teach the greatest principles. And if you follow these correctly, they will make our faith invincible. Practicing that which is permissible with these we make paradise admissible. So, remember the Almighty and practice spiritual principle.

Do not fall from a life of bliss. And the truth do not twist. For this type of conduct everlasting life, you will be have missed. So, this type of lifestyle we should always resist. And with truth and patience the believers do exist.

The truth is like a brick house built to last for thousands of years. It has always been around. Many have come and many have gone with lies they continue to expound. However, with truth our feet are firmly planted on the ground. And the truth of the Almighty will always be a beautiful sound.

THE GIFT OF THE ALMIGHTY

The Gift of the Almighty will bring you honor and glory. And your children and grandchildren, nieces and nephews, will hear your beautiful story. The gift does not come in a hurry. The gift is so precious that you can be certain that you will never have to worry.

Early one morning while drinking a glass of tea. I opened a spiritual book and it began talking to me. So, I write this message hoping you can see that the spiritual life will guide you to your true destiny. It will help you live successfully.

Never take for granted the truth that you have been taught. because with blood, sweat, and tears, this truth has been sought. This truth is so special and so precious that it can never be bought. but it can only be passed on and it will never leave you distraught.

TO THE ALMIGHTY WE PRAY

It is only to the Almighty that we pray, asking for forgiveness and thanking him for another day. Do this and you will never sway or be engaged in unimportant play. And consider your deeds for by them you will live to see another day. And the spiritual things will help you find your way.

OK as you continue to move towards your goal it is something that only you can control. With the Almighty, we can preserve and save our soul. Pray that your spiritual eyes are open so that you can see that blessed knowledge of a higher goal.

Those who betrayed you, and those who look down on you will one day need you. The truth be told you will be able to fulfill that need. What will you do? Treat them better than they have treated you.

BEING REAL

Being real comes with ups and downs, wins and losses, failures and successes, and sometimes years of scars. Do not allow anyone to define who you are nor what you believe in and what you stand for.

Can you ask forgiveness for your sins? Do you think that you have been forgiven? With every day that begins we look forward to another opportunity to ask forgiveness for our sin. Remember the Almighty forgives again and again.

Never forget true devotion to the Almighty. Which will give us a wonderful day. A day when true life begins. Remain devoted to the end.

NEVER FORSAKE THE TRUTH

Never forsake the truth because in our heart it has been planted. Nor take it for granted. Contemplate on it and expand it. Study the universal laws that the Almighty has commanded. And on solid ground your feet will be supplanted.

And on that glorious day true values will be restored, and your gifts and treasures would be more. And those who look to the Almighty, countless miracles will be poured. Waiting on that glorious day, doing things the spiritual way.

The believers have everlasting life as the ultimate prize. And to many this will be a pleasant surprise. And many will be losers because of their lies.

However, truth to the believer the Almighty has supplied. And soon all of us will arrive thankful to be alive.

WHERE YOU PUT YOUR EYES

Be careful where you put your eyes because it could lead to your demise. And by the eyes one can become hypnotized. Always keep your eyes on the prize. And with the Almighty you will be the one who survives.

The message of the Almighty is clear to those who try and understand. And as you reach toward him, he will take your hand. Spiritual things will become clear and you will see that your deliverance is very near.

There is nothing more profound than a spiritual turn around. Returning your feet to solid ground. And now thanks to the Almighty a new life you have found.

GRACE AND FAVOR

The Almighty bestows grace and favor according to his will and plan. Renew your mind and take your stand, help the orphan when you can. And you will have success, again and again.

There is always a struggle and a fight when your intentions are to do right. Sometime the fight is in the day and sometimes it is in the night. But it is not important because the Almighty will give you a brilliant light. And to his rope hold on tight.

This life is short in time. Therefore, continue forward spiritually and continue to climb, continue to enjoy your life and find some sunshine. And continue to focus on the Almighty the divine.

NO MORE EMOTIONAL PAIN

The Almighty is the cure to all social and emotional pain. However, with faith and endurance peace you will obtain. With everlasting life in your heavenly domain.

By the Almighty my life from the world was transferred. You gave me a spiritual book, your holy word. And now I am free like the bird, because of the spiritual voices that I heard.

Spiritual poetry gives me more. And with these words they help me to open many doors, spreading truth from shore to shore. Thanking the Almighty for being alive. And reading his word is like eating honey straight from the beehive. And with inspirational knowledge is how we survive.

Made in the USA
Columbia, SC
20 November 2024